DISTANCE TO FENCES

	FEET	METERS
Left Field	315	96
Left Center Field	379	115.5
Center Field	390	118.9
Deep Center Field	420	128
Deep Right Field	380	115.8
Right Field	302	92

HEIGHT OF FENCE

	FEET	METERS
Left Field Wall	37	11.3
(In addition, screen extends 23 feet, or 7 meters)		
Center Field Wall	17	5.2
Bullpens	5	1.5
Right Field	3 to 5	.9 to 1.5

FENWAY PARK GROUND RULES

Foul poles, screen poles, and screen on top of left-field fence are outside of playing field.

Batted ball going through scoreboard, either on the bound or fly: 2 bases.

Fly ball striking anywhere between left center-field wall and right of line behind flagpole: home run.

Fly ball striking wall or flagpole and bounding into bleachers: home run.

Fly ball striking line or right of same on wall in right center: home run.

Fly ball striking right center-field wall left of line and bounding into bullpen: home run.

Batted ball sticking in bullpen screen: 2 bases.

Batted or thrown ball remaining behind or under canvas or in cylinder: 2 bases.

Batted ball striking bevel on the wall between the foul pole in left field and the corner in back of the flagpole, and bounding into stands or out of park: 2 bases.

Batted ball striking top of scoreboard, also ladder below top of wall and bounding out of the park: 2 bases.

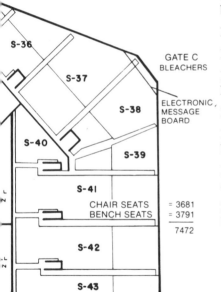

GATE C
BLEACHERS

ELECTRONIC
MESSAGE
BOARD

CHAIR SEATS = 3681
BENCH SEATS = 3791
—————
7472

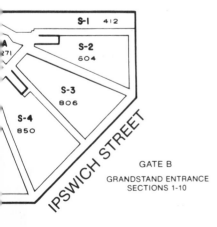

WITHDRAWN

S-1 412
S-2 604
S-3 806
S-4 850

271

GATE B
GRANDSTAND ENTRANCE
SECTIONS 1-10

IPSWICH STREET

WITHDRAWN

THE BALLPARK

One Day Behind the Scenes at a Major League Game

THE BALLPARK

BY
WILLIAM JASPERSOHN

LITTLE BROWN AND CO.
BOSTON/TORONTO

Also by William Jaspersohn
A DAY IN THE LIFE OF A VETERINARIAN

Library of Congress Cataloging in Publication Data

Jaspersohn, William.
　The Ballpark

　　SUMARY: A behind-the-scenes view of Fenway Park,
home of the Boston Red Sox.
　　1. Boston, Fenway Park—Juvenile literature.
2. Boston. Baseball club (American League)—Juvenile
literature. [1. Boston. Fenway Park. 2. Boston.
Baseball club (American League)] I. Title.
GV875.B62J37　　　796.357'068'0974461　　　79–22835
ISBN 0–316–45812–0
ISBN 0–316–45811–2 pbk.

M

Published simultaneously in Canada
by Little, Brown & Company (Canada) Limited

PRINTED IN THE UNITED STATES OF AMERICA

For my parents,
Paul Jaspersohn
and
Dorothy Dickson Daley Jaspersohn

. . . and for all the other coaches
along the way

Preface

The home of baseball's Boston Red Sox, Fenway Park is nearly seventy years old. Yet, despite inevitable changes in its appearance over the years, including the addition of an electronic message board in 1976, it has retained its essential character as an old-fashioned brick-and-steel ballpark. It is one of a dying breed, however. Of nearly twenty ballparks that were more than thirty years old in 1957, it is one of only five* still in use. The others have been torn down or abandoned.

Thus, the day-to-day life of a Fenway Park is of more than usual interest, I think, especially in this antiseptic era of AstroTurf and air-conditioned sports domes. In telling the story of Fenway Park on the day of a game, I have deliberately sidestepped the subjects of baseball trades and finance, which are complex and interesting enough to warrant definitive treatment by themselves. And though the cast of characters on these pages will in time undoubtedly change, they were the people present at the ballpark when I was preparing this book. For the reader like myself who has always wondered what happens before, during, and after a game, I hope this book helps explain how a ballpark really works.

---

*The other stadiums still in use are White Sox (formerly Comisky) Park (1910) and Wrigley Field (1914) in Chicago; Tiger (formerly Briggs) Stadium (1912) in Detroit; and Yankee Stadium (1923) in New York.

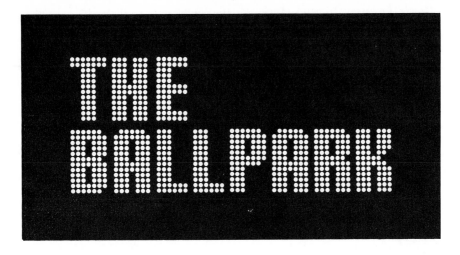

THE BALLPARK

One Day Behind the Scenes at a Major League Game

A ballpark is never quite empty.

At 6 A.M., the pigeons in Fenway Park stir from their roosts in the rafters under the grandstands and, fluttering, drop for crumbs of popcorn under the brightly painted seats. The June air is windless, the sky, blue above the spacious fan-shaped field, and mist clings to the brushed emerald grass.

2   The ballpark is quiet. But the hush will soon be broken

because there's a baseball game today. At two-fifteen, the Boston Red Sox will play the Kansas City Royals. Thirty-five thousand people will view the game in the park. Two million more people will watch it on television. For Fenway Park's five hundred employees the day will be long and hard. But for the moment a restful silence fills the seats and the ballpark shimmers greenly under a warm dawn sun.

On any morning throughout the year, whether there's a baseball game or not, the first workers to arrive at the park are the ground-crew members. They are in charge of grooming the field and maintaining the ballpark overall. At 7 A.M., thirteen of them assemble along the third baseline to "dump" the vinyl tarpaulin that has been covering the infield all night. "Dumping the tarp" is ground-crew language for getting all the rainwater and condensation off it, and the ground crew does this by folding the tarp over and hauling it into right field to dry. It takes at least six people to move the tarp, because even when dry it weighs over one ton.

Then, out at the center-field flagpole, two ground-crew members raise the huge flag, which is twelve feet wide and eighteen feet long. Besides serving its patriotic function, the billowing flag helps fielders figure which way the wind is blowing, and how to judge the paths of fly balls.

At seven-thirty the park's commissary opens. That's where the refreshments and souvenirs that are sold throughout the park are stored and prepared. Fenway Park's concessions are run by a private firm, the Harry M. Stevens Company, and the department manager's name is Rico Picardi. He has worked in Fenway Park's commissary since 1943. On the morning of a game day his first task is deciding how much food should be prepared.

Jack Lyons runs the souvenir department, which stocks all the pennants, T-shirts, caps, baseballs, mugs, dolls, bats, posters, and other items for the park's nine souvenir stands. Pennants always sell well, and for a big game like today's, Jack likes to make sure that enough are on hand.

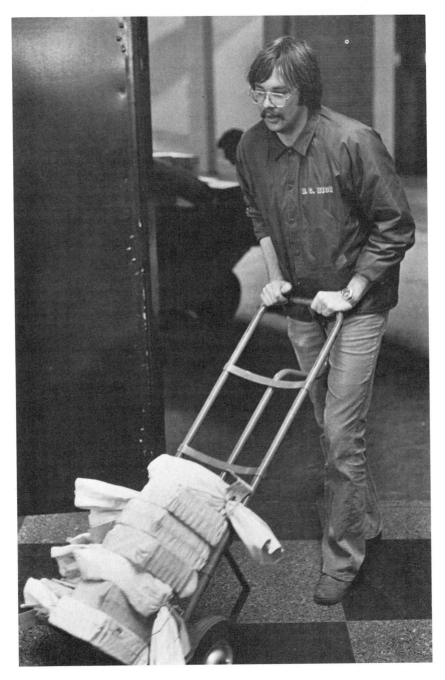

Soon, the change for the vendors who sell souvenirs and refreshments in the grandstands arrives from a bank by truck. The man who wheels the bags of change to the commissary safe is Jack Burns. He is in charge of the vendors. He gives them their selling assignments, supervises them during games, and afterward makes sure they account for everything they've sold. Like many Stevens supervisors, he was a commissary worker himself once.

7

Within minutes after the commissary opens, trucks start rolling up outside the park's service gate with all kinds of deliveries marked FENWAY PARK. From food wholesalers throughout Boston come sacks of sugar, popcorn, and coffee, and cartons of frankfurters, buns, ketchup, mustard, chicken, hamburgers, pizza, ice cream, soda, candy bars, French fries, and milk. From warehouses come kegs of beer and cartons of cigarettes, and boxes of paper plates, cups, napkins, and towels, and cellophane, toilet paper, soap, sponges, squeegees, brooms, and mops. From the printers come stacks of the day's programs, freshly inked and stapled. In fact, even a truckload of birch dowels gets delivered. These come from a wood mill in northern Vermont and will be used as pennant sticks.

Soon more employees start showing up for work, and the
ballpark takes on an air of bustle.

In the commissary, workers are packing thousands of frankfurters in buns for the vendors to sell this afternoon. The franks are then run through a machine that wraps them in cellophane to keep them fresh until they are cooked. During a game, the franks and buns that the vendors sell are cooked in their wrappers in three connecting microwave ovens. Franks sold in the snack bars are steamed.

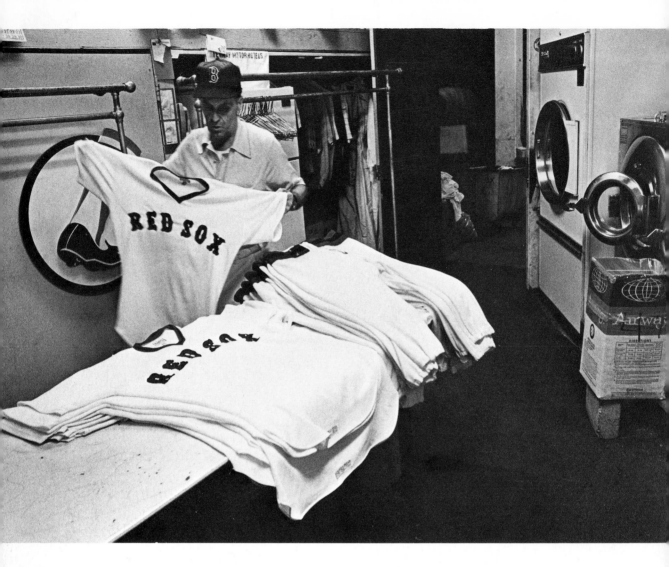

One of the busier places on the morning of a game day is the laundry room, which is located under the grandstands on the third-base side of the park. There, a senior ground-crew member, John P. McGonagle, washes the Red Sox uniforms that will be worn for today's game. Until a few years ago, major league baseball uniforms were made of wool and had to be cleaned at a dry cleaner's. Today they are made of a machine-washable double-knit material that teams can wash themselves and that doesn't need ironing. They are expensive, though. A new Red Sox uniform costs over one hundred fifty dollars, and each player is assigned six of them: three white uniforms with RED SOX stitched on the shirts for home games, and three gray ones with BOSTON stitched on the shirts for away games.

John P. McGonagle doesn't like drying the uniforms by machine — he says that they don't come out smelling fresh. So instead, as soon as they're washed, he hangs them on racks and wheels them through a door under the grandstands to dry in left field.

While the food is prepared and the laundry gets done, the ground crew is hard at work, grooming the field for today's game. Every one of the forty ground-crew members has a special job for getting the field and grandstands in shape.

Sonny Billings drives the tooth harrow, a machine that digs up the topsoil on the basepaths, so that afterward rakers can rake it flat. The chief purpose of the ground crew is to make the field as level and smooth as possible so that conditions for playing baseball are near-perfect.

The rakers and other ground-crew members are supervised by Joe Mooney, the superintendent of grounds and maintenance. Joe's ground-crew experience goes back many years. As a teenager he worked on ground crews in Scranton, Pennsylvania, and for ten years before coming to Fenway Park he was superintendent of grounds and maintenance at Robert F. Kennedy Stadium in Washington, D.C.

The basepaths at Fenway Park are covered with a mixture of topsoil and a water-absorbent substance called Turface. The grass is Merion bluegrass, which is well-suited to the harsh New England climate. At least every other day, whether the Red Sox are playing at home or not, the ground crew mows the infield grass to a height of one-half inch, and the outfield grass to a height of one inch. Between mowings, the grass is watered and fertilized.

Weather information is vital to the work of a ground crew. Joe Mooney receives weather reports from a government weather station in Bedford, Massachusetts. Last night Bedford forecast showers for the Boston area, so yesterday, before they went home, the ground crew removed the iron caps from the more than fifty drain holes in the park to collect whatever rain fell on the field. The holes drained the rainwater into pipes permanently buried throughout the outfield and around home plate, and the pipes filtered the water into the ground. If the drain holes hadn't been opened, there would have been puddles everywhere when the ground crew arrived this morning.

Now ground-crew member O. B. O'Brien recaps the holes
and carefully covers the caps with earth and Turface so
that outfielders won't step in them later and twist their
ankles.

The rest of the ground crew is busy, too. Out in left field, Brian Sullivan readies the scoreboard for today's game, while nearby, Warner Jackson scrubs the bases. These are bought in sets of three, and each set costs one hundred five dollars.

Once the infield has been raked, it is rolled and watered to pack it slightly and keep down the dust. Then Al Forester can set the bases and lay the baselines, and Charlie Freni can paint home plate.

Jim McCarthy grooms the pitcher's mound. It takes one hour to get the mound ready, and the hardest part is landscaping it so that it slopes evenly toward home plate. The pitching rubber on which the pitcher stands is mounted on a buried slab of concrete. To give pitchers the firmest possible surface to pitch from, Jim packs the space in front of the rubber with balls of red clay, which he flattens into place with an iron tamper. Then, when everything is raked and smooth, he tacks down a rubber mat to protect the mound during batting practice.

The last big morning chore for the ground crew is folding the tarpaulin, which has been drying in right field, and rolling it onto its steel cylinder. The tarpaulin covers the infield from mid-March until the end of the season in early October. The only time it is not used during this period is when the Red Sox are on road trips. During games, the tarpaulin is stored on its cylinder along the first baseline near a place where the ground crew sits called *canvas alley.*

In April, before the baseball season begins, the ground crew has practice sessions called *tarp drills,* so that if it rains during a game, they're prepared to cover the infield quickly, before it gets soaked. When everyone does his job correctly, the crew can spread the huge tarp in less than two minutes.

By ten o'clock, the field is almost ready for batting practice. Now, on the ballpark roof, the television cameras that will televise today's game are installed by a technical crew from station WSBK–TV, Boston. One camera is placed on each of the two narrow walkways called *slings,* located on the left and right sides of the roof. One is placed in the broadcast booth for a view from behind home plate. And one is placed on a wooden platform near the center-field flagpole for a view from behind the pitcher.

National and local networks have their own permanent cables at the ballpark for sending sound and picture signals back to their home stations. The stations then broadcast the signals by transmitter to their audience's television sets.

While the outdoor work has been going on, a truck has arrived from the airport with a very special cargo: the uniforms, bats, and other equipment of the Kansas City Royals. The truck parks outside the place where visiting teams dress, called the *visiting-team clubhouse*, and a crew quickly unloads the trunks and bags.

Inside the clubhouse, Fenway Park's visiting-team equipment manager, Don "Fitzie" Fitzpatrick, unpacks the bags and hangs each player's uniform in its assigned locker. Fitzie's job consists mainly in keeping the visitors' clubhouse organized, and seeing that the visiting players are well provided. He has been with the Red Sox a long time. In 1944, he was one of the team batboys. Some players, he says, are superstitious about which locker they're assigned, so he keeps a chart to make sure they get the same one each time.

He hangs the manager's uniform in the visiting-team manager's office.

Sometimes ball players forget little things when they go on road trips, such as combs, razors, shaving lotions, and hair sprays. So most home teams, including the Red Sox, supply various toiletries for visiting players.

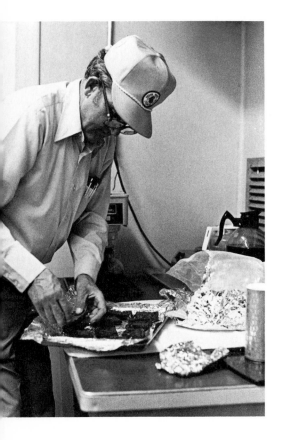

All major league clubhouses have a locker room, a
training room (for treating aches and bruises), a manager's
office, bathrooms, and showers. Fenway Park's clubhouses
also have laundry rooms, soda bars, and snack counters.
Ball players appreciate home-baked goods, so for every
home game, Fitzie's sister, Mary St. Sauver, bakes a fresh
batch of brownies for the visiting team.

For now all Fitzie has left to do is brew some coffee and
refill the candy and bubble gum jars. Within an hour, the
Kansas City Royals, who flew in to Boston last night,
should be arriving on foot or by taxi from their hotel.

Meanwhile, in the Red Sox clubhouse, the home-team equipment manager, Vinnie Orlando, puts fresh fruit out for the Red Sox team. Most Red Sox players like coffee and doughnuts in the morning before a game, so Vinnie stocks the clubhouse snack counter with those items, too. After a game he always serves a meal to the team, usually stew, lasagna, or barbecued ribs. The food, which comes from the commissary, is kept hot in portable steam tables.

A few minutes later, two clubhouse helpers, Tommy Cremens and Joey Cocuzzo, arrive from left field with the dry uniforms. Vinnie quickly hangs them in their proper places.

Tommy Cremens is the Red Sox batboy. His main job is taking care of the Red Sox batting gear and the baseballs during a game, but he has other duties, too. In the clubhouse he runs errands for the players, and cleans their spiked shoes, and helps Vinnie hang their uniforms. Before the players arrive, he always sorts their white undersocks, or *sanitaries*, and puts a pair in each player's locker. And when the bags belonging to the day's umpires arrive by truck from the airport, he carries them upstairs to the umpires' dressing room.

A new batboy is recommended for the job by the previous one, and then, after a short tryout, if the players and equipment manager like the new boy, he is hired. Tommy has been batboy for the Red Sox for two seasons. The rest of the time he is a college student.

The Red Sox hire two batboys, one for themselves, and one for the visiting team when their regular batboy isn't with them. Batboys are usually allowed to travel with their teams only once a season, and this year Tommy went with the Red Sox to California. In Anaheim, he got to see Disneyland.

Tommy says the hardest part of his job is doubleheaders because they last so long, and Butch Lewis, the visiting-team batboy, agrees. During a game, the batboy has to sit on one knee near the on-deck circle, make sure the players get the right bats, and keep the home plate umpire supplied with baseballs. Since some players are superstitious about batting, the batboy must learn quickly whether they like their bats left in the bat rack or brought to the on-deck circle.

It is 10:30 A.M. Since nine o'clock people have been buying tickets in the advance sales ticket office on Jersey Street. In April the ticket department makes estimates based on the Red Sox schedule of how many people to expect for each of the eighty-one home games. Then only that number of tickets is printed. If more tickets are needed, they can be printed and delivered in one day.

An important part of the ticket sellers' job is knowing exactly where to find any ticket for any game.

The reserved seat tickets for today's game against the Royals have been sold out for weeks, but people are still telephoning this morning to find out if any are left. The woman who answers the calls is Helen Robinson, "the voice of the Red Sox switchboard." She has been operator and receptionist at Fenway Park for thirty-five years.

She pushes a button. *Click.* "Red Sox!"

"Hello," says the caller. "Are there any tickets left for today's game?"

"Only bleacher seat tickets which go on sale at noon, sir."

"Thank you very much."

"You're welcome." *Click.* "Red Sox! . . ."

By two this afternoon Helen will have answered more than one thousand such calls.

Upstairs from Helen in Fenway Park's executive offices, Haywood Sullivan and Edward "Buddy" LeRoux are hard at work. Mr. Sullivan, or Sully, as his staff calls him, is general manager of the Red Sox, and as such is in charge of the entire ball-playing operation. He oversees the Red Sox major and minor league teams, hires scouts, players, and managers, and makes trades for new players with other teams. As vice-president of the Red Sox, Mr. LeRoux handles all the financial business of the ballpark, such as selling radio and television rights of home games to networks, and buying new equipment for the Red Sox team.

On the morning of a game day both men like to arrive early at the ballpark and work at their desks for a few hours. But later this afternoon they will be at the game, watching from their private boxes on the ballpark roof.

Another person who will be at the game is Joe McDermott, who is special assistant to Mr. Sullivan and Mr. LeRoux. One of his main jobs is organizing all the ushers, ticket takers, crowd control staff, and security people so that every part of the ballpark is properly policed. To keep track of where these groups are assigned, Joe marks their stations with colored pushpins on a map of the park called a *schematic*.

The ushers, who will help people find their seats at today's game, come to work at ten forty-five. Ushers are assigned to sections of the park on a seniority basis, and lists are posted of who will be working on a given day. In all, there are eighty ushers. They change into their red jackets, blue slacks, and blue caps in a locker room near the visiting-team clubhouse.

In the commissary, the vendors, who will sell refreshments at today's game, start signing in for work, too. Tom Foley is a high school student who has been a vendor at Fenway Park since he was fourteen years old. He is seventeen now. By law you must be at least fourteen years of age to sell food at Fenway Park, and at least twenty-one to sell beer in the concession stands.

The vendors' locker room is right next door to the ushers'. For night games, which start at seven-thirty, vendors must be suited up by six, and during the school year, Tom finds himself rushed to finish his homework.

The most important arrivals, of course, are the players themselves. All the Red Sox players drive to work and park their cars in a small, fenced-in lot outside the Red Sox clubhouse. At eleven o'clock the lot attendants, Steve McGrath and Jerry Clarke, spot the first player's car coming up Van Ness Street toward the ballpark.

The driver is Bob Stanley, one of the ten pitchers on the Red Sox staff. A minute later, Butch Hobson, the Red Sox third baseman, arrives in his silver and maroon pickup truck. And then in their various vehicles come Jim Rice, Mike Torrez, Carlton Fisk, Rick Burleson, Jerry Remy, Fred Lynn, Carl Yastrzemski, Dwight Evans, Dennis Eckersley, and all the rest of the Red Sox players and coaches. They quickly enter a side door that leads to the Red Sox clubhouse.

41

There, each team member has an individual box for his mail, and a second box for storing money and other valuables for safekeeping. After picking up their mail and depositing their valuables, the players and coaches fill out forms for complimentary tickets, or *comps* as they're called. By the terms of his contract, each Red Sox player is entitled to six comps per home game, but if he needs more — for family, relatives, or friends — he can usually borrow extras from teammates not using all of theirs.

Mike Torrez isn't pitching today, but he still needs all his comps for family and friends.

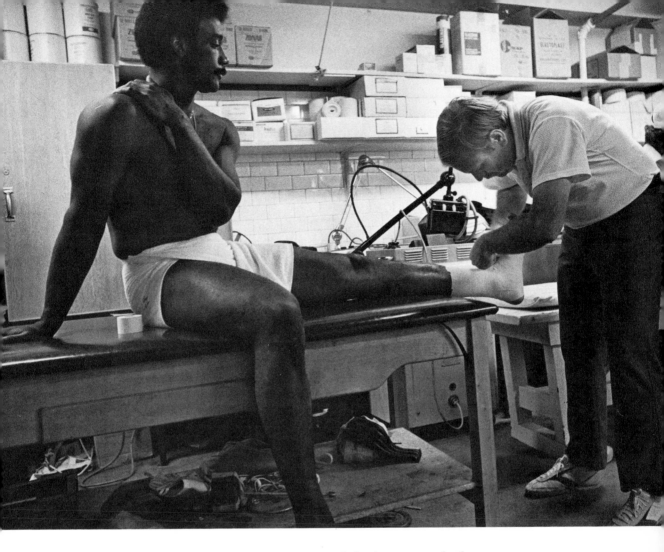

Then, after they change out of their street clothes, some of the players go to a kind of infirmary called the *training room* to see the Red Sox trainer, Charlie Moss. Charlie studied to be an athletic trainer at the University of Arizona, and worked as head trainer at Northeastern University before coming to the Red Sox in 1975. A major league trainer's job includes traveling with the team, treating players' injuries, massaging arms and legs, and generally helping players with their health needs. During games, Charlie sits with the Red Sox in their dugout so he is near the field and ready to give first aid if a player is injured. For serious injuries, all major league teams have team physicians. The Red Sox have two, who also supervise the park's first aid stations.

Now Charlie tapes the ankles of outfielder Jim Rice as a protective measure against twists and sprains.

43

Before batting practice, some players like to work out on the weight machines in a private room across from the clubhouse called the *Nautilus room*. Bob Stanley often uses a machine for toning up his chest, arm, and shoulder muscles, while Dwight Evans, the Red Sox right fielder, works out on the leg exerciser. Throughout the year players work hard at staying in shape, and several Red Sox players have weight machines in their homes.

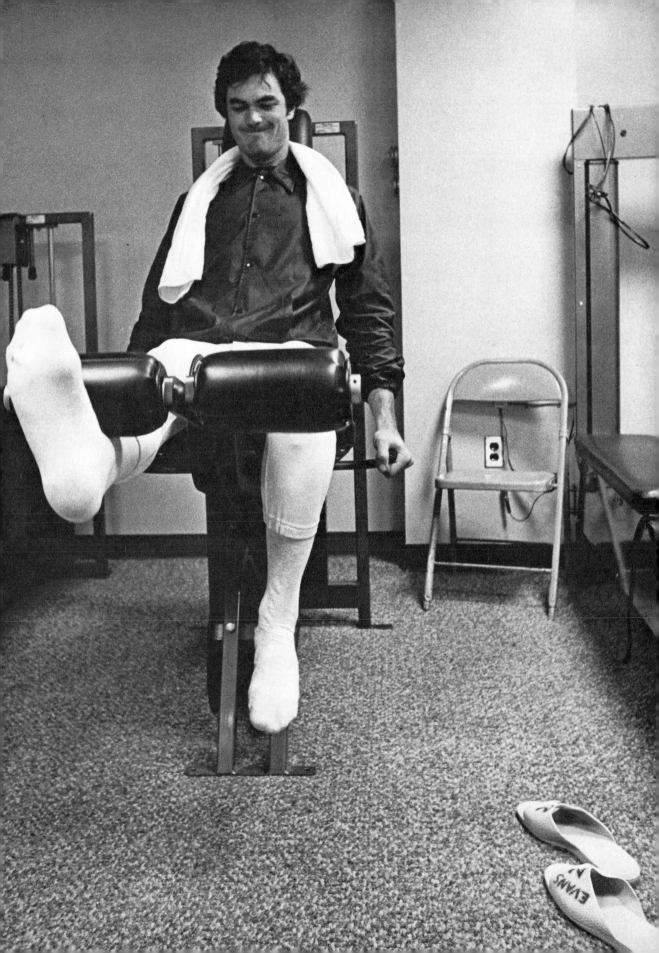

Next door in a tiny space called the *video room*, players can watch videotapes of past games on special television monitors. Jim Rice goes there today to study his batting style with one of the Red Sox coaches, Johnny Pesky.

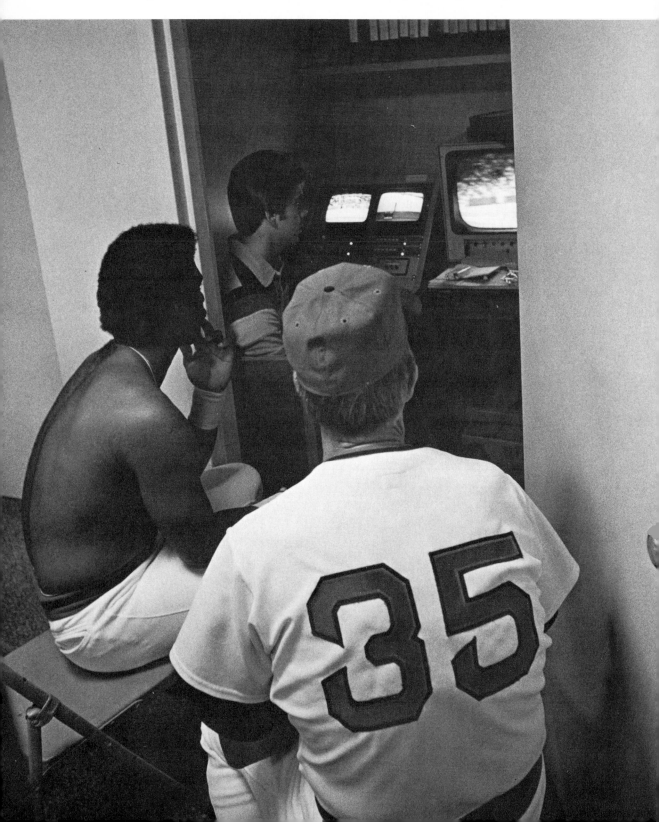

In the clubhouse itself, most players are having coffee, chatting, or just trying to relax. Mike Torrez autographs a dozen baseballs that will eventually be signed by every team member, then given as souvenirs by Mike to his friends.

Other players have different routines, depending on whether they are playing this afternoon. Carl Yastrzemski, the Red Sox captain, chooses his bats for today's game. All major league batters have their bats made to order by private bat-making companies, usually either Adirondack or Hillerich and Bradsby. The bats are made of ash wood, and the type Yaz prefers weighs thirty-five ounces. Every season Yaz can expect to go through a dozen bats, for which the Red Sox pay the bill. To save his best bats for games, Yaz uses a different set for batting practice. Between games, all bats are stored in the clubhouse on steel racks. 47

At eleven-fifty, the whole team, including Butch Hobson, the Red Sox third baseman, and Carlton Fisk, the catcher, is dressed and ready for work. Now, in ones and twos, the players walk down a flight of carpeted steps from the clubhouse and through a long tunnel and out through the dugout to batting practice.

While the team was getting dressed, the ground crew put rope screens in front of the dugouts, the pitcher's mound, and first and second bases. These screens protect players and spectators from stray balls hit or thrown during batting practice. A portable aluminum structure known as a *batting cage* was erected behind home plate. From here each player takes four practice bunts and ten swings at bat.

Each batting practice is usually pitched by three or four team members. One such person is Al Jackson, who is also the Red Sox pitching coach. Al played on the original New York Mets team in 1961, and later pitched for the St. Louis Cardinals.

Some fans say that batting practice isn't worth the effort, but batters such as Dwight Evans will tell you that it helps sharpen your timing at the plate, and also warms you up.   51

On the sidelines near first and second base another kind of warmup is in progress: a "pepper" game between Johnny Pesky and relief pitchers Bill Campbell and Tom Burgmeier. During games, relief pitchers for both teams sit in center-field enclosures for warmup throwing called *bullpens*. Since a relief pitcher never knows when he might pitch, he must be in shape and ready at all times. After this pepper game, these pitchers will run wind sprints, catch fly balls, and do calisthenics in the outfield.

The chief spectators at a Red Sox batting practice are ushers, vendors, and baseball reporters. Batting practice is really a vendor's only time to see the team in action because during the game he is too busy selling refreshments to watch.

The baseball reporters work for newspapers, television, radio, or magazines. For them, batting practice is a perfect time to interview players on any baseball-related subjects. Press passes are issued by the Red Sox public relations office, and these passes allow the reporters on the field until ten minutes before game time. Reporters conduct their interviews in the dugout or near the batting cage as players await their turns at bat.

Today a radio reporter is taping a story on the differences between major and minor league baseball. He asks Fred Lynn, the Red Sox center fielder, to comment: "Generally," says Fred, "the fields, the lighting, and the overall playing conditions are better in the majors, as well as the quality of play. In the minors, if you're a good hitter, pitchers will pitch around you to go after the poorer hitters. In the majors, where you've got guys behind you who can hit, pitchers can't afford to do that."

"What's the toughest part of being a major league player?" asks the reporter.

"Well," says Fred, "it's not so much the travel itself, as being away from your family. There are eighty-one road games a season, and eighty-one days is a long time to be away from people you love."

"What do you do when you aren't playing baseball?" asks the reporter.

"I go fishing," says Fred. "There are a number of rivers near where I live, and I like to fish for bass."

"Thank you," says the reporter.

By noon all the ballpark's one hundred fifty concession workers have arrived for work. Danny Lapin and his wife Linda set up the souvenir stand under the grandstands behind home plate. In the off season Danny works as a chemical salesman, but he's been a concession worker at Fenway Park for twenty-two years. The souvenirs for his stand come from a supply room in the commissary, and nothing can be removed unless it's signed for. At the end of a day Danny returns whatever items haven't sold, then folds up his portable stand.

The same system of sign-outs is used for distributing food among the eighteen snack bars throughout the park. Boys assigned as *porters* bring allotments of food on wagons from the commissary refrigerators to the snack bars. But before the food can be put away, the snack bars must be thoroughly scrubbed and hosed.

Now all the ushers, ticket takers, vendors, and concession workers go to their assigned places. Only ten minutes remain before the gates are unlocked at twelve-thirty.

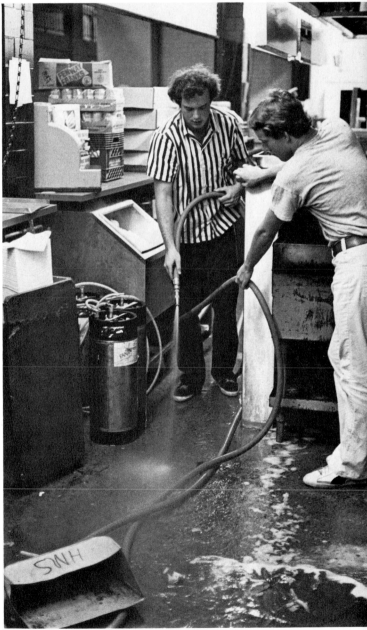

Outside the ballpark the sidewalks are swarming with people awaiting the opening of the gates. Many are families who live in or near Boston, but others are Red Sox or Royals fans who have come hundreds of miles just to see today's game. Among the day's spectators are a movie actress, a United States senator, a famous football quarterback, and the governor of a large midwestern state. All these dignitaries are already inside the park, brought through a special entrance near the players' parking lot.

Finally, at twelve-thirty, supervisors around the park shout, "Open 'em up, boys!" The ticket takers unlock the gates, and the crowd starts to stream in. The day's attendance is computed by the ticket department from the total number of tickets sold. But to keep track of how many people actually enter the ballpark, counting devices called *turnstyles* are located inside the gates.

On a busy afternoon a single ticket taker may collect as many as three thousand tickets at one gate.

Inside the park one of the first employees the public encounters is Al Green, who mans the information booth behind home plate. Besides giving seating information, Al looks after lost items and lost children. Usually four or five wallets are turned in to him after a game, along with radios, eyeglasses, pocketbooks, cameras, binoculars, suitcases, books, umbrellas, sweaters, jackets, and briefcases. Most items are claimed the same day by their owners, but whatever isn't claimed is left upstairs with Helen Robinson at the reception desk.

During any game Al can expect to see twelve or more lost children. On youth days, when many children are in the park, he can expect to see at least fifty. Most of them don't have their tickets and can't remember where they were sitting. Al asks them to wait near the booth, and eventually someone comes by and claims them.

In the grandstands ushers are showing people to their seats. Tickets are marked by section, row, and seat number, and using this system an usher can quickly locate any seat in the park.

Once the crowd starts arriving, Jack Burns gathers the vendors together outside the commissary and reads them their day's selling assignments. Tom Foley gets assigned to sell franks, which are being cooked at this moment in the commissary microwave ovens.

After the franks are cooked they are packed sixty to a batch in lightweight aluminum chests, which are stacked and ready when the vendors enter the commissary. On cold days portable heaters are placed inside the chests to keep the franks hot.

Before leaving with a chest, each vendor gives Jack a plastic token so he can keep track of how many food chests are taken.

Then for Tom and the other eighty vendors, it's up the ramps and into the stands for a long afternoon of selling.

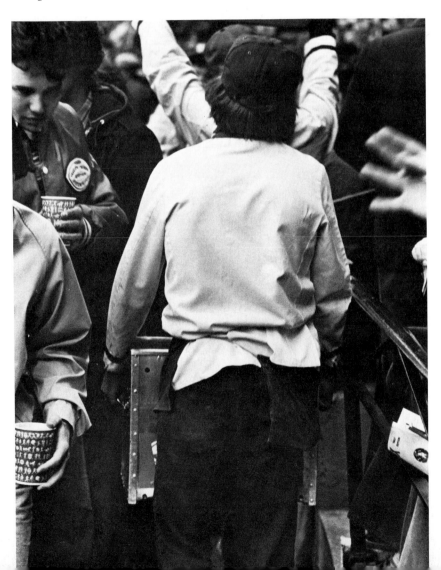

By twelve forty-five the Red Sox have finished batting practice, and the Royals have taken the field. Most Red Sox players now return through the tunnel to the clubhouse to change their uniforms, rest, and cool off. Some stay in the dugout to answer reporters' questions. A few, like Johnny Pesky and Dennis Eckersley, sign autographs for the fans near the field. Team members generally don't mind signing autographs, unless they are busy, or the team just lost.

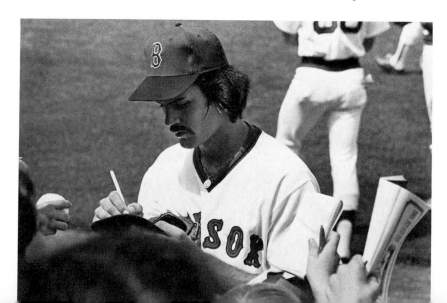

When reporters finish questioning the players, they go
upstairs through the grandstands and check in at the press
gate on the ballpark roof. There, the press usher, Richie
Howard, has a list from public relations of every person
allowed that day into the rooftop viewing area known as
the *pressbox*. Now he checks in a newspaper reporter
named Peter Gammons, who covers baseball for the Boston
Globe.

At this hour, while the visiting team bats, the pressbox
and broadcast booths are relatively quiet. In the WSBK
television booth, Joan Mulcahy, an assistant director for
the station, uses the opportunity to arrange the message
cards that will be read on the air this afternoon.

After they check in, all reporters and other media people
break for lunch in the press dining room across from the
pressbox.

Meanwhile, the umpires wait upstairs in their locker room until game time at two-fifteen. The umpires work for no team but are paid by the American League of Professional Baseball, whose offices are in New York City. The league gives the men their umpiring assignments, pays them a food, travel, and lodging allowance, and makes their reservations from city to city. Normally, umpires officiate a series of games between two teams, but sometimes, like today, they work only one game before moving on to another city.

Terry Cooney has been an American League umpire for five years. Today he will umpire at home plate. The home plate umpire is in charge of the game balls, which are always supplied by the home team. On his arrival at the park, Terry received sixty game baseballs and a satchel to put them in from Red Sox equipment manager, Vinnie Orlando. To make the baseballs more visible and less slippery, major league umpires rub them with a special mud from near the Delaware River. The mud, which is finely sifted and very silty, has been used by the major leagues for years, and a single can costs fifteen dollars.

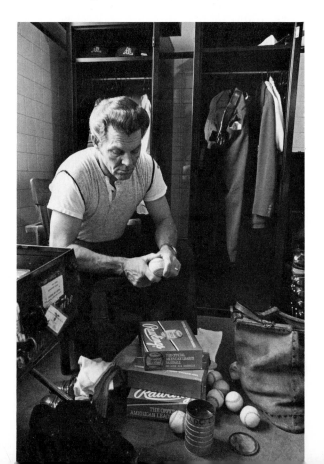

The other umpires today are Al Clark, Hank Soar, and Bill Kunkel. Major league umpires receive their training at umpires' schools and by umpiring in the minor leagues. Al Clark, for example, took the Umpires' Specialization Course at Saint Petersburg, Florida. For four years he umpired in the Midwest, Texas, American Association, and Venezuelan Winter Leagues before joining the American League in 1976.

A good umpire must possess good judgment and good hand–eye coordination. Major league umpires will tell you that the hardest part of their job is not the officiating itself, but the travel — living in hotel rooms, eating restaurant food, and being away from their families for seven months of the year.

Al Clark says people sometimes forget that umpires don't care which team wins or loses. "We don't have favorite teams," he says. "When umpires make mistakes, they are 100 percent honest mistakes."

It is almost two o'clock. The ground crew now grooms the field once more and gives the basepaths a final hosing. The crowd is seated, thirty-five thousand strong, and both teams are in their dugouts, warmed up and ready.

Under the left-field grandstand, Al Forester, one of the senior ground-crew members, readies the bullpen cart for its afternoon's work. The cart is used during games to chauffeur relief pitchers from the bullpen to the infield when they are summoned to pitch. Seven heavy-duty batteries power the cart, which was specially made for the Red Sox by a company in California.

During games the cart is parked near the ground-crew's bench in canvas alley. An electrical charger which Al packs with him is attached to the batteries to keep them charged at all times.

Most major league ballparks have organists who play music for the spectators. Fenway Park's organist, John Kiley, is also the organist at the Boston Garden during the hockey and basketball seasons. John sits in a glass booth behind the announcer's table in the pressbox, and his view 70 to the field is perfect.

At two-fifteen the Red Sox take the field, and the public-address announcer says, "Ladies and gentlemen, will you all please rise and sing our National Anthem?" And everyone stands and sings as John plays "The Star-Spangled Banner."

Then Terry Cooney sweeps home plate with a tiny pocket broom, snaps on his mask, and shouts, "Play ball!" The Red Sox pitcher, Jim Wright, dusts his hands with a sticky powder called *rosin* to rid them of excess perspiration. The rosin comes from a porous cloth bag placed on the mound a moment earlier by Tommy Cremens.

Finally, seven hours and twenty-one minutes after the ground crew dumped the tarp, Jim Wright steps up on the smooth, flawless mound. Carlton Fisk waits for Wright to lean in, then flicks him the sign: one finger. Pudge wants a fastball. Wright lays his first two fingers across the seams of the baseball and winds up and throws the first pitch. It's a strike. The crowd roars. The game has begun.

73

As the game gets under way, two groups watching closely are the reporters in the pressbox and the photographers in the photographers' dugout. There are one hundred eighteen seats in the pressbox, and room for eight photographers in the photographers' dugout. The places for both groups are assigned by the Red Sox public relations office.

The reporters make note of each play in special scorebooks which they later use as references when they write their accounts of the game.

Like the reporters, the photographers usually work for magazines or newspapers, and their job is to shoot action pictures of the game. Their cameras are equipped with long lenses called *telephoto lenses*, which work like telescopes to focus on any action in the field. Devices known as *motor drives* advance the film in their cameras automatically, which enables the photographers to shoot up to three pictures per second.

The person in the pressbox watching the game closest of all is the *official scorer*. He is the one who officially records every play of the game. An official scorer cannot call balls, strikes, or outs, or declare a batted ball fair or foul. Those are an umpire's duties. But he is the person who rules on hits and errors, and the order of action in any play.

To be an official scorer in the major leagues you must be a member of the Baseball Writers' Association of America for at least four years, and must attend at least one hundred baseball games a season.

Today's official scorer, Joe Giuliotti, is a sportswriter for the Boston *Herald American*. When he rules on a close play, his decision is announced to the rest of the press members over a closed-circuit address system. The man who makes the announcements, Bill Crowley, is the Red Sox public relations director.

76

Whatever statistics appear in reporters' stories, such as batting averages and strikeout totals, come from statistics sheets, or *stats* as they're called. The Red Sox front office keeps computerized records of every American League player's averages. Before each game, those of the Red Sox and the day's opponent are printed and distributed as stats to each reporter. The man who distributes the stats is Tom McCarthy, the pressbox *steward*. He has been with the Red Sox for forty-three years. One reporter he sees at nearly every game is Bob Ryan, who writes for the Boston *Globe*.

When reporters get thirsty, they go to a counter in the back of the pressbox where they can get free beverages.

At the announcer's table in a separate room in the pressbox called the *control room* sits Sherman Feller, the Red Sox public-address announcer. Besides introducing the various players to the crowd and making announcements, Sherm runs the balls-and-strikes section of the left-field scoreboard. Wires running from the scoreboard and along the grandstand roof lead to a control panel on the announcer's table. For every ball or strike, Sherm flips a different switch on the panel and a colored bulb lights up on the scoreboard.

The score itself is posted from inside the scoreboard by a
ground-crew member named Ronnie Thompson. Before the
game Ronnie entered the scoreboard through a door in its
left side. During the game he can watch the action from
different peepholes. As runs are scored, he takes down the
appropriate steel card from its peg and slides it through the
correct slot in the scoreboard.

Many fans at the ballpark want to know the scores of other games being played today, so these are received in the control room on a device called a *ticker-tape machine*. It is watched by a ground-crew member named Kevin Harrison. As scores come in, Kevin telephones Ronnie, who posts them on a separate part of the scoreboard. In turn, after each inning Kevin phones the score of the Red Sox game to a sports ticker office in New York, which transmits his report to ticker-tape machines in other ballparks.

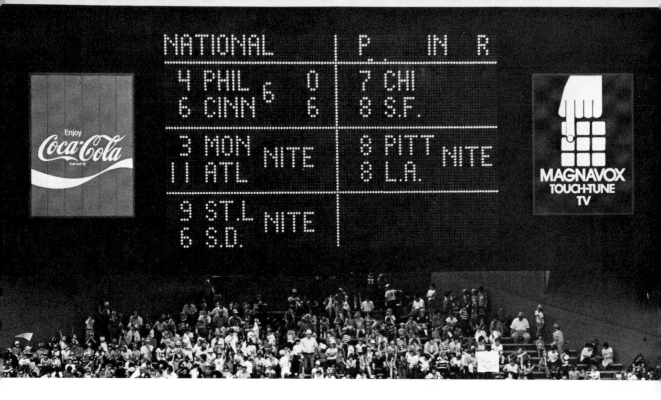

NATIONAL   P,   IN   R

4 PHIL   0   7 CHI
6 CINN   6   6   8 S.F.

3 MON   NITE   8 PITT   NITE
11 ATL   8 L.A.

9 ST.L   NITE
6 S.D.

Enjoy Coca-Cola

MAGNAVOX TOUCH-TUNE TV

Some of the scores are posted with other messages on an *electronic message board* above the center-field bleachers. The messages are typed in the pressbox control room on machines known as *terminals*, then transferred to the board by the push of a button. The terminal operators are Bill Gutfarb and Steve Hug.

For information such as players' batting averages, the board and terminals are connected to a computer in Fenway Park's accounting office. Photos and statistics of every American League player, along with other messages, are stored on a special disc, which Bill installs in the computer before each game. To show a player's batting average during a game, Bill types a code on his terminal into the computer, and instantly the player's picture, name, and average appear on the board.

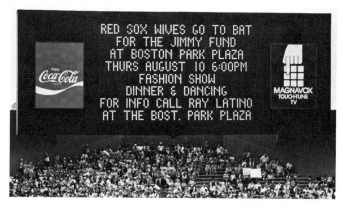

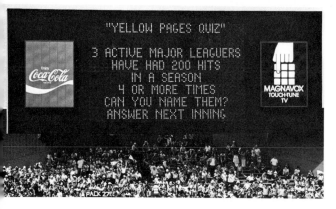

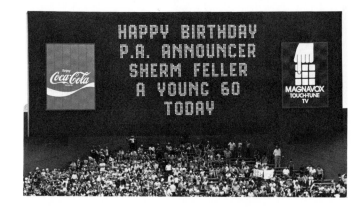

Behind the terminals an electronic panel called a *video console* is ready to feed the board film, slides, videotapes, pictures, and animations as they are needed. Jim Healey, who works in the Red Sox public relations office, is the console operator. For instant replays of any game action, the console is connected to WSBK–TV's broadcast equipment. Jim needs only to push two buttons, and the message board shows the replay immediately.

To catch any action missed by WSBK, the message board has its own television camera, which sits in the sling on the third-base side of the park. It is operated by one of several ground-crew members, who wears headphones and takes orders from Jim Healey in the control room.

Like many Red Sox employees, Dick Bresciani, the team's assistant public relations director, has a second job at the ballpark, that of *statistician*. During games he sits in the control room keeping score, and later he analyzes the data with the help of the computer. Statistics help teams understand what their strengths and weaknesses are and why they are winning or losing.

In the booths below the pressbox and control room, radio and television crews are broadcasting today's game to millions of people throughout the Northeast.

The radio announcers are Rico Petrocelli and Ken Coleman, who work for station WITS in Boston. Baseball radio announcers must *ad lib* almost everything they say, that is, speak without notes or preparation. For some announcers the hardest time to ad lib is during rain delays, because then they must keep talking even though the game is stopped. Ken and Rico, however, actually enjoy rain delays, because, as Ken says, "It gives us a chance to loosen up and be a little more ourselves for a while."

From the microphones into which Ken and Rico speak, their voices travel as electrical waves to a special console behind them called an *amplifier*. This device strengthens the electrical waves, which travel by wire to the WITS transmitter in Boston. From there, they are broadcast to the radio audience. The commercial messages, which are mostly prerecorded on tape, are broadcast directly from the station.

Inside the WSBK television booth, announcers Ned Martin and Ken Harrelson are also commenting on today's game. They take cues from Joan Mulcahy, who signals them when they're on the air and also hands them message cards to read.

At the same time, the four WSBK television cameras that were installed this morning are capturing all the action down on the field.

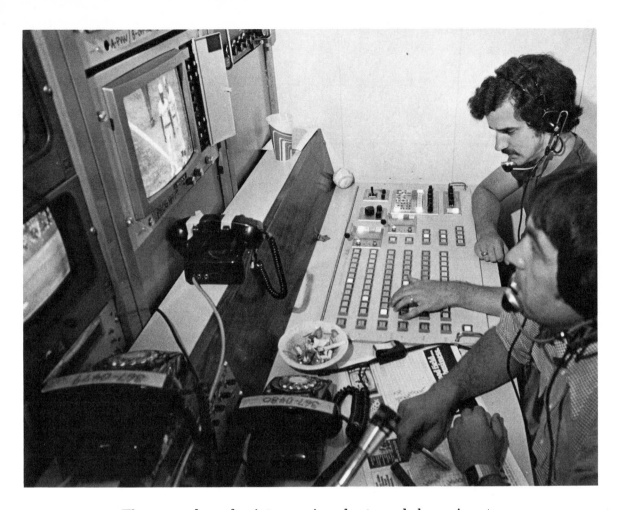

The sound and picture signals travel by wire to a television truck in the rear of the players' parking lot. From a control room inside the truck the WSBK director, Tommy Todisco, manages the telecast of the game. Television monitors show Tommy the pictures being taken by each of the four cameras inside the park. To telecast a certain camera's picture he calls out its number, and the *switcher* sitting next to him pushes a button, putting that camera on the air. The sound and picture signals then are beamed by microwave to the home station, which broadcasts the signals to its audience.

In addition to the switcher, Tommy is assisted by an *audio engineer*, who controls the sound levels of the announcers' microphones; a *video engineer*, who adjusts the pictures that come from the cameras; and a *"slo-mo" engineer*, who operates the slow motion and instant replay equipment.

89

By the third inning, the score remains tied at 0–0, and it looks as if Jim Wright and the Royals pitcher, Dennis Leonard, are locked into a real pitchers' duel.

Between innings, spectators rush down the ramps for refreshments, and the porters push by with fresh supplies of food for the jam-packed snack bars.

In the grandstands, the vendors are doing a brisk business, too. Tom Foley has already sold three chests' worth of franks, and the game isn't even half over. Vendors are paid a commission on everything they sell, and on a good day selling franks, Tom says he can earn between twenty and thirty dollars.

When vendors run out of franks, they return to the commissary where workers have more of them freshly cooked and waiting.

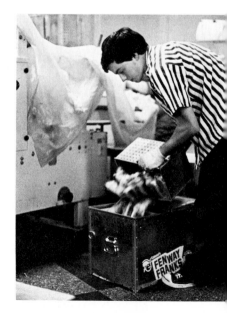

The soft drink vendors also return to the commissary for fresh supplies of cola. A worker fills a wire rack with twenty paper cups, then puts the rack under a metal board that has a hole for each cup. By dumping a measured load of crushed ice across the top of the board, he can fill all twenty cups at once with ice. Then he passes the rack under a row of spigots that fill the cups with cola five at a time. When the cups are full, another worker puts them under a capping machine which seals them with cellophane caps.

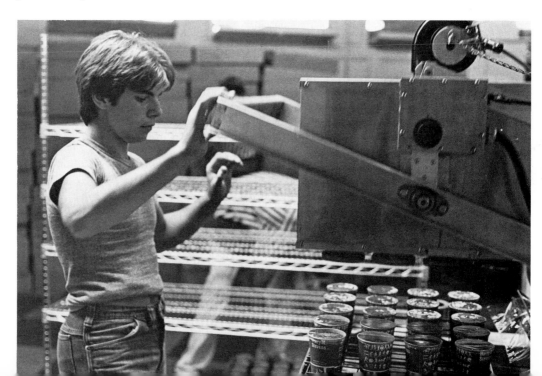

Meanwhile, the popcorn vendors are getting their refills from one of two popcorn rooms, out under the bleachers or near the commissary. The popcorn, which was popped and bagged this morning, is stored in lofts above the rooms until ready to be used. During the game two workers are assigned to each room. While one of them tosses down the bags, the other fills rack upon rack with paper popcorn horns.

The racks are then placed four at a time on a bench, and a stainless steel board with a hole for each horn is lowered on top. The worker dumps one bag of popcorn over the board and spreads it across the holes with a rubber paddle. The popcorn drops through the holes and into the horns, and the racks, filled and ready, are placed on shelves for the vendors to take. Unlike some ballpark refreshments, such as ice cream, which doesn't sell well in cold weather, popcorn is always a big seller. Today the whole supply in this room will be exhausted.

In the fourth inning, with two outs and a runner on second base, the Red Sox center fielder, Fred Lynn, hits a sharp double off the right-field wall that drives in the first run of the game. The crowd, which until now has been attentive but quiet, goes wild.

While the fans cheer and cheer, twelve young men known as the *crowd control squad* are patrolling the ballpark for any signs of unruliness. The squad works with the city police, the ushers, and a private security force to maintain order in the ballpark at all times. In case of a problem, squad members can summon each other for help on walkie-talkie radios.

98

People come to baseball games for pleasure and excitement, but there is no room at a ballpark for any kind of unruliness. If a spectator is disorderly — if he gets drunk, starts a fight, smokes marijuana, or destroys park property — the crowd control squad has the power of management to confiscate the offender's ticket and eject him from the ballpark immediately. And if a spectator runs onto the field during a game, he is arrested, locked in the city jail for the night, and the next day taken to court and fined one hundred twenty-five dollars. Despite these penalties, some six spectators a season are arrested for breaking this rule.

Besides policing the ballpark, the various security squads also watch for spectators who might be lost, sick, or injured. At almost every game, at least one spectator is struck by a foul ball, and others may suffer heart attacks, falls, strokes, seizures, or, like one woman today, a fainting spell. Spectators with medical problems are taken to one of two first aid rooms under the grandstands on the first- and third-base sides of the park. There, four nurses are ready with the necessary first aid treatment. Patients with serious problems are seen by the team physicians, and, if necessary, rushed by the Fenway Park ambulance to a nearby hospital.

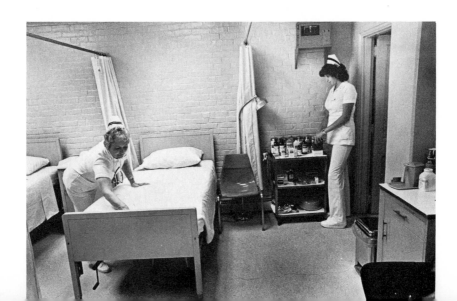

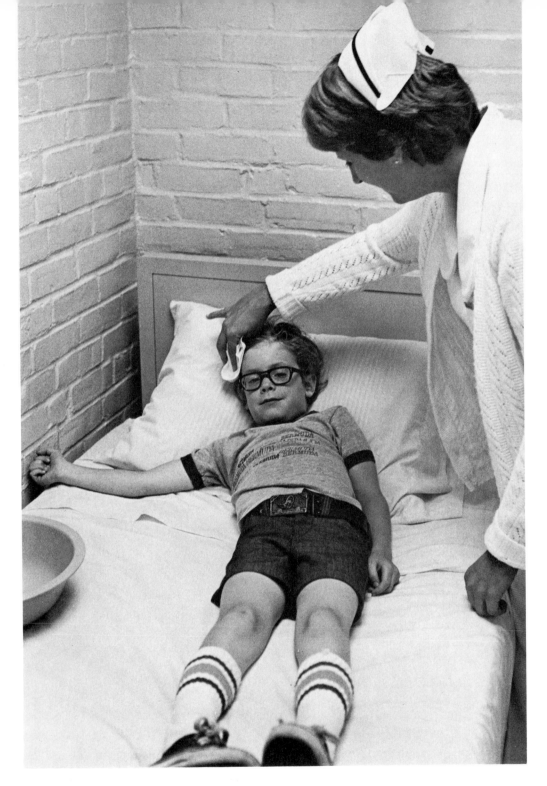

Ryan Kelleher came one hundred miles with his parents to see today's game, his first ever. But in the fifth inning he developed a stomachache, and his parents brought him to the first aid room to rest. Now, two innings later, he says he's feeling much better, and wants to return to his seat.

The game, meanwhile, is moving to an exciting close. In the bottom of the eighth inning and still behind by one run, Kansas City stops a Boston rally. Then, in the top of the ninth, with two outs and Royals runners on first and third, Butch Hobson stabs a hard ground ball hit by a Royals infielder and throws it to second baseman Jerry Remy for the final out. The fans roar. The Red Sox have won the game, 1–0, behind the strong six-hit pitching of Jim Wright. The team is happy and relieved. After congratulating their pitcher they disappear down the dugout tunnel and into the quiet of the clubhouse. At the same time, ushers and policemen jump from the stands and surround the field to prevent spectators from coming onto it.

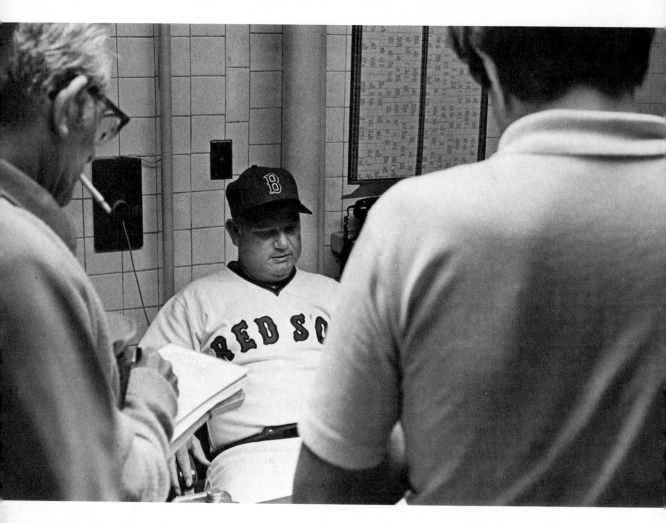

For a few minutes after a game the only people in the clubhouse are the players, the coaches, and the clubhouse staff. But then the reporters, who have come downstairs from the pressbox, enter the clubhouse for postgame interviews with some of the team. They traditionally start by interviewing the Red Sox manager, Don Zimmer, in his office adjacent to the clubhouse. They ask his opinion of the game — of the pitching, the hitting, and the fielding. Zim patiently answers each question, then the reporters troop through the clubhouse to speak with some of the players.

Many reporters interview Jim Wright because he pitched so well, and they want to quote him in their news stories. Clark Booth interviews Carlton Fisk for television. Clark's summary of the game, including excerpts from this interview, will be broadcast tonight on his station's evening news program.

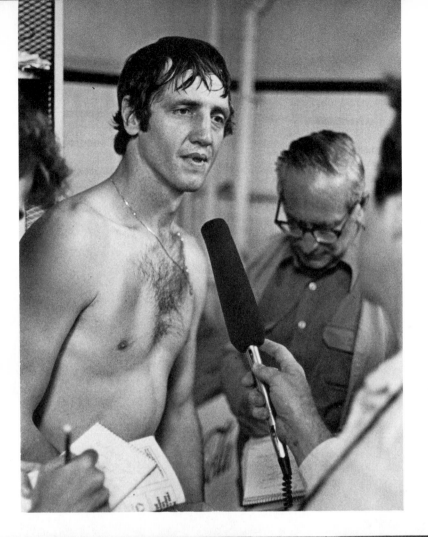

While the players meet the press, the clubhouse staff packs the team equipment for a game tomorrow night in Baltimore. Everything the team will need on the road, including uniforms, bats, and gloves, is packed in a special bag or trunk.

Tommy Cremens packs the sunglasses worn by Red Sox fielders that can be flipped up away from the eyes when not needed. For road trips these glasses travel in a compartmentalized trunk.

The players' caps are packed in a special suitcase so that they won't be crushed. And whatever bats each player wants on the trip are packed in two oversized trunks.

In just a few minutes a truck will drive the equipment to the airport. And a bus will drive the team as soon as everyone has showered and dressed.

It is almost five-thirty. The grandstands, only minutes ago thronged with spectators, have emptied. Out in the bleachers a private clean-up crew has begun the long and difficult task of cleaning the entire ballpark. Twenty-five workers known as *pickers* walk between the seats with giant bags, picking up paper and other bulky debris. This allows ten men with gasoline-powered blowing machines strapped to their backs to blow the lighter trash down to the bottom of the stands. There it is shoveled into barrels by workers called *pick-up men*, and dumped into garbage trucks outside the park.

In all, it takes the crew eight hours to clean the ballpark, and when it rains the wet trash makes the job even longer. After night games the crew usually start their cleaning around midnight, and if they're lucky, they finish by dawn.

Tomorrow, while the Red Sox play in Baltimore, the clean-up crew will return to hose the seats and runways so that the ballpark is washed and fresh for the next home game, in three days.

In the pressbox, some reporters have returned from interviewing the players and are hastily writing their stories about the game for tomorrow's newspapers. Baseball writers, especially those who work for newspapers, write under the pressure of *deadlines*, so to write faster they all compose their stories on typewriters. Usually, from the time they leave the clubhouse and sit down and start typing, the newspaper reporters have an hour to finish their stories, which might run a thousand words long.

Joe Fitzgerald writes sports features for the Boston *Herald American*. Today he is writing a six-hundred-word feature on Jim Rice for tomorrow's sports page. The job will take him fifty-five minutes.

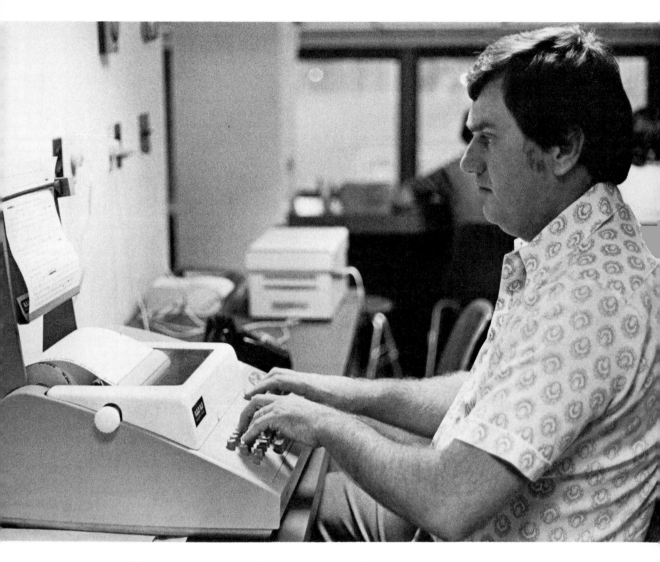

After a story is written, it must be sent to the reporter's newspaper office as fast as possible for printing. A sports story written in Fenway Park is usually handed to one of several teletypists at the back of the pressbox. He types it on a device called a *teletypewriter*. From there the story travels by wire to a second teletypewriter back at the reporter's newspaper office, where it is edited for grammatical mistakes and for length, then sent to the pressroom and printed in tomorrow's newspaper.

Richie Dolan has been a teletypist for twenty-two years. During the hockey and basketball seasons he operates a teletypewriter at the Boston Garden. He can type one hundred words a minute, but says he must type slower because the machine can print only sixty-five.

At 6:30 P.M., the Red Sox team walks from their clubhouse and through their parking lot to a waiting bus. From Fenway Park they will go to Logan Airport, where a charter jetliner is waiting to fly them to Baltimore. The only other passengers will be the team's traveling secretary, who booked the flight; the team statistician, Dick Bresciani; and a handful of baseball reporters.

In the plane the players will sit two to a row with an empty seat between them, as stipulated in their contracts. Once in flight they will dine on steak, baked potato, peas, rolls, salad, and ice cream. After supper some team members will doze. Others will read, play cards, or listen to music on their portable cassette players.

In Baltimore a bus will drive the team to their hotel where they will sleep one to a room. Most players will sleep late tomorrow, but some will rise early and go sightseeing, while others will sit in the hotel lobby and read. At four tomorrow afternoon a bus will drive them to the Orioles ballpark where their equipment will be already unpacked and in lockers.

The Red Sox will play the Orioles two nights in a row. After the second game, the team will board a plane and fly back to Boston, arriving at Logan at three in the morning. The whole team will be exhausted, but everyone will drive to his home and go to bed . . . only to awaken for another game that night.

114

Now, as the bus leaves Fenway Park, a cheer goes up for the team from fans who have gathered at the gate. Many fans wave, and the players, from inside the bus, wave back.

Inside the ballpark the field and the seats are dark. The gates are locked. The numbers have been taken down from the scoreboard, and the Kansas City Royals, now dressed and packed, have left for the airport, too.

A great stillness presses down on the field.

A baseball game was played here today before 35,109 people, but few of those fans could have guessed all the work involved to produce the game they saw.

The Red Sox will return. But before they do, the Fenway Park staff will make sure that everything is ready for their next home stand. For the past twelve hours the workers have done their jobs well, and now the last remaining group in the park is the clean-up crew. The noise of their blowers cuts up again through the silence of the grandstands.

The ballpark is almost empty.

Acknowledgments

Literally hundreds of people were helpful in the preparation of this book. I especially wish to thank Jim Healey of the Boston Red Sox public relations office, who arranged for me to photograph in various areas of the ballpark, tirelessly answered all my questions, proofread my manuscript, and encouraged me from beginning to end. Over the course of the book's development, I came to regard Jim not only as a helpful liaison, but also as a friend. Too, this book would not have been possible without the help and cooperation of Bill Crowley, vice-president of Red Sox public relations, who was the first to hear about and clear the way for the project, and who introduced me to Jim. Dick Bresciani, team public relations director, was my liaison with the Red Sox team. Tommy Harper, former Red Sox player and now an administrative assistant for the club, informally briefed me from his own experience on the day-to-day life of a professional ball player. Mary Jane Ryan, also with public relations, prepared my press passes from game to game, and was an indispensable source of information about the park.

I am deeply grateful to both Haywood Sullivan and Edward LeRoux for taking time out from their busy schedules to allow me to photograph them for this book. Meeting them both was a privilege and an honor beyond measure.

The rest of the Fenway Park staff was kind and cooperative, too, particularly the players and coaches. Special thanks to Joe McDermott, executive assistant for the club and a fine photographer in his own right; and to Jim Oliver, team treasurer; Ed Kenney, farm-team director; Helen Robinson, switchboard operator and receptionist; Jerry Buckley, team photographer; Sherman Feller, team public-address announcer; and particularly Bill Gutfarb, computer engineer and scoreboard operator, who lent me useful notes about the park, and also taught me something about computers. Don Fitzpatrick was always helpful when I was working in the clubhouse, as were Vince Orlando, Charlie Moss, Tommy Cremens, Eddie Kennedy, Richie Connolly, Joey Cocuzzo, Butch Lewis, Danny Ahearn, and Ronnie Hankerson. My great good thanks to Carl Yastrzemski, Carlton Fisk, Dwight Evans, Bob Stanley, Fred Lynn, Butch Hobson, Jerry Remy, Mike Torrez, Jim Wright, Jim Rice, and the rest of the Red Sox team for their very special cooperation. And I am indebted to Joe Mooney of the grounds and maintenance department; Rico Picardi, Jack Lyons, and Jack Burns of the concession department; Arthur Moscato of the ticket department; Amby Anderson of the ushers' crew: Betty Gray, Diane Dawkins, Irene Parr, and Pat Lynch of the nurses' stations; Mark Sweeney of crowd control; Captain Ed Horton of security; Jack DiAngelis of the clean-up crew; and all their fine, friendly staffs for letting me photograph them at work.

Bryan Burns of the Kansas City Royals public relations office read the manuscript of this book, and was my liaison with the Royals club. Dick Beach, program director for station WSBK–TV, Boston, paved the way for my photographing the TV–38 remote crew. My thanks also to Gloria Gibson of WITS radio and Arthur Fischer of Ogden Security, Boston, for their exceedingly kind cooperation.

One of the nicest parts of my experience at the ballpark was meeting those stalwarts, the reporters, photographers, and media crews. My deep thanks to Peter Gammons and Bob Ryan of the Boston *Globe*; Joe Fitzgerald, Joe Giuliotti, Ted Gartland, and Ted Ancher of the Boston *Herald American*; Joe Karas, Don Kalischer, Mike Sciosia, Glenn Sauer, Joe Hughes, George Niakaros, Tommy Todisco, Jack Fortnat, Joan Mulcahy, Ken Harrelson, and Ned Martin of WSBK–TV; Rico Petrocelli and Art Roberts of WITS radio; Ken Coleman, executive director of the Jimmy Fund, and also with WITS; Harold Rich of the Providence *Journal*; Clark Booth of WCVB–TV, Boston; Jim Huie and Alan Henderson of NBC Sports; John Vallante of Amfax Communications,

Boston; and Richie Dolan of Western Union, Boston, for allowing me a glimpse into their dazzling and hectic world.

Another group that deserves special acknowledgment are the umpires who appear in these pages: Bill Kunkel, Terry Cooney, Al Clark, and Hank Soar; and their supervisor, Dick Butler of the American League Umpires' Office. Through Mr. Clark and Mr. Butler I was able to contact the family and associates of the late Lena Blackburn, the legendary pitching coach for the Chicago White Sox who developed the silky mud still rubbed on every baseball in the major leagues. For those baseball aficionados who wonder about the origins of this mythical mud, I can only report that, contrary to popular belief, neither the Delaware River nor Rancocas Creek is its turbid source.

Before embarking on this book I reread John Updike's brilliant homage to Ted Williams, "Hub Fans Bid Kid Adieu," in Mr. Updike's *Assorted Prose*. Among its many delights, the piece contains for me one of the most phenomenologically correct evocations of a baseball game ever written, and in its opening paragraph a perfect verbal miniature of Fenway Park. For those wishing information on the history and lore of Fenway Park, I recommend Melvin Maddocks's fine article, "All You Ever Wanted in a Ballpark — and Less" in the September 15, 1975 issue of *Sports Illustrated*. And while pennants flutter elsewhere in the American League, I continue to find solace in Roger Angell's loving analysis of the 1975 World Series in his splendid book, *Five Seasons*.

Once again, I owe an enormous debt of gratitude to my friend Ward Rice of The Camera Store, Stowe, Vermont, who, with his usual exactitude and grace, printed the photographs for this book.

I am extremely grateful, too, that my editor at Little, Brown is John Keller, a man of enormous energy, dedication, talent, and good cheer — and also an avid baseball enthusiast. John helped guide and sustain me through every phase of this book, and in the best and truest sense of the word, this book is ours.

My warm appreciation also to the rest of the children's book staff at Little, Brown, especially Bob Lowe, who designed this book, Claude Lee, Peggy Freudenthal, and that transplanted Vermonter, Felice Forrest.

Leslie Welch of Pioneer Printers and Dan Price of Wordgraphics, both in Stowe, Vermont, performed yeomanlike graphics and retouching work for this book, and Freda Moody lent a helpful hand.

Do an author's friends and relatives know what aid and comfort they give him? My affectionate thanks to the following people for their very special support: Thelma Backels, Susan Butler, Bill and Joan Canby, Hayden Carruth, Peter Cunningham, Pete and Jan Cunningham, Sonny Davis, John Dostal, Steve and Joan Geller, Steve and Donna Good, Steele Griswold, Jim and Penny Hommeyer, Paul Jaspersohn, Ron and Chris Jaspersohn, Alex Johnson, Michael Katzenberg, Len and Betsy Langer, Alan and Kathy Lindsey, David Luce, Charlie and Anne Lusk, Molly Lusk, Alan and Pat Morton, Don Nelson, Bud and Sadie Packard, Kenny Paul, Richard Rachals, Dan Rea, Linda Rice, Robbie Rice, Petya Rostova, George Salambier, Eric and Amy Schulz, Chris Scobie, David and Jane Sequist, Bert Shook, Bridget Steers, Saskia Swenson, Victor and Sarah Swenson, Zoe Swenson, Gene Touchette, Frank and Margaret Willing, Frank and Betty Woods, Miles Wright.

Finally, love and thanks to Pam, baseball lover nonpareil, for everything, everything else.

FENWAY PARK

BOSTON RED SOX

Constructed 1912, Rebuilt 1934

SEATING CAPACITY:

Roof Boxes	594
Lower Boxes	4,085
Upper Boxes	6,479
Grandstands	14,927
Bleachers	7,420
Total	33,505

ATTENDANCE RECORDS

Record Crowd: 41,766 (New York, 2 games, August 12, 1934)
Post-War and Single Game Record: 36,350 (New York, August 7, 1956)
Record Crowd since 1956: 35,939 (New York, May 31, 1976, night)
Night Game All-time Record: 36,228 (New York, June 28, 1949)
Opening Day Record: 35,343 (Baltimore, April 14, 1969)

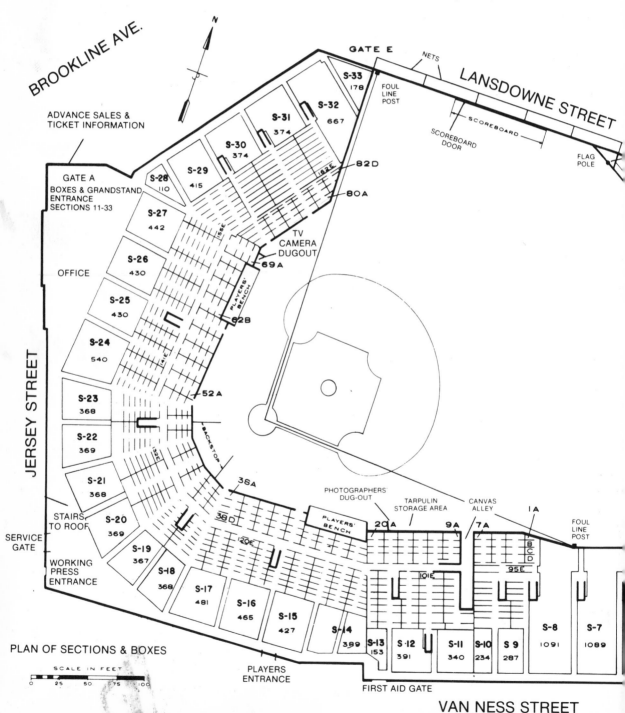

PLAN OF SECTIONS & BOXES